PERSONAL SUCCESS

BRIAN TRACY

AMACOM AMERICAN MANAGEMENT ASSOCIATION

New York • Atlanta • Brussels • Chicago • Mexico City
San Francisco • Shanghai • Tokyo • Toronto • Washington, D.C.

Library of Congress Cataloging-in-Publication Data
Tracy, Brian, author.
Personal success / Brian Tracy.
    pages cm
Includes index.
ISBN 978-0-8144-3703-2 (hardcover) — ISBN 978-0-8144-3704-9 (ebook)   1. Career development. 2. Executive ability. 3. Promotions. 4. Success in business. I. Title.
HF5381.T653 2016
650.1—dc23
                                                              2015030402

About AMA

American Management Association (www.amanet.org) is a world leader in talent development, advancing the skills of individuals to drive business success. Our mission is to support the goals of individuals and organizations through a complete range of products and services, including classroom and virtual seminars, webcasts, webinars, podcasts, conferences, corporate and government solutions, business books, and research. AMA's approach to improving performance combines experiential learning—learning through doing—with opportunities for ongoing professional growth at every step of one's career journey.

Printing number
10 9 8 7 6 5 4 3 2 1

CONTENTS

Introduction   1

1 Obey the Laws   4

2 Decide Exactly What You Want   10

3 Develop the Habits of Courage and Self-Confidence   15

4 Be True to Yourself   19

5 Develop a Positive Mental Attitude   24

6 Communicate Positively and Expect the Best   29

7 Develop a Bias for Action   34

8 Satisfy Your Most Important Customers   38

9 Be a Hard Worker   43

10 Dedicate Yourself to Continuous Learning   48

11 Become a Competent Speaker 53

12 Associate with the Right People 58

13 Network Continually 63

14 Knowledge Is Power 68

15 Dress for Success 73

16 Commit to Excellence 78

17 Plan Strategically 82

18 Accept Responsibility for Results 85

19 Be a Team Player 89

20 Develop Your Creativity 92

21 Put Fortune on Your Side 97

SUMMARY Three Keys to Success 101

Index 105

Introduction

WHY ARE some people more successful in their careers than others? Why do some people grow and flourish, get promoted more often, move ahead rapidly, and enjoy greater satisfaction in their life and work?

Is the person who earns $250,000 per year ten times smarter, better, or more capable than a person who earns $25,000 per year? Of course not! In a research study, 1,000 adults were given standard IQ tests. The most intelligent person in the sample was only 2.5 times smarter than the least intelligent person in the group. The income difference, however, was astonishing! The highest-paid person in the sample was earning 100 times more than the income of the lowest-paid person in the sample.

Here is another important point. The highest-paid person in the sample was not the most intelligent in terms of IQ. The lowest-paid person in the sample was not the least intelligent. Up to a certain point, intelligence, or raw natural talent, had something to do with the success or lack of success of the individual. But after that, it came down to personal qualities, hard work, continuous learning, and excellent time management.

The Winning Edge Concept

The Pareto principle states that the top 20 percent of income earners take in 80 percent of the total income in any business or industry. Meanwhile, the bottom 80 percent of income earners share only 20 percent of the total income. Why does this happen?

After many years of research and study, we finally have the answers to these questions. The starting point is called the "winning edge concept," which says that small, marginal differences in competence in vital areas can translate into enormous differences in results. This concept also states that small weaknesses in critical areas can, in themselves, be sufficient to keep individuals at low levels of achievement and income, year after year, whether or not they are aware of those weaknesses.

If a horse runs in a horse race and comes in first by a nose, it wins ten times the prize money of the horse that comes in second, by a nose. Does this mean that the horse that comes in first by a nose is ten times faster than the second-place horse? Of course not. Is the winning horse five times faster or 50 percent faster? Is it 10 percent faster? No, the difference between the winners and the losers, the famous champions and the has-beens who are forgotten to history, is only about 3 percent in the critical areas.

Achieving Elite Performance

In his work on elite performance, K. Anders Ericsson found that the people at the top of any field were characterized by having invested more time over their careers to hone their most important skills, while the others had not.

There is an excellent quote from Henry Wadsworth Longfellow that describes the most successful people of every age:

> Those heights by great men, won and kept,
> Were not achieved by sudden flight;
> But they, while their companions slept,
> Were toiling upward in the night.

Everything Counts

This book contains twenty-one ideas that you can use to begin developing the key requirements for personal success, while simultaneously ridding yourself of deficiencies that may be holding you back.

This book is based on the Law of Accumulation, which says that "everything counts!" Everything you do on a day-to-day basis, every decision you make, every action you take or fail to take, accumulates over time and ultimately manifests in your success, or lack thereof.

Consistent application of the ideas in this book can lead you to greater success, faster than you ever imagined possible. Let's begin.

ONE

Obey the Laws

IN 350 BC, at a time when people believed in the gods of Mount Olympus and in luck, coincidences, and random acts of fate, Aristotle postulated his *principle of causality*. He said that there are no random events. There is a cause-and-effect relationship between everything that happens. Even if we do not know the causes, they do exist.

Everything that happens to you or for you in your life happens for specific causes, which lead to the effects that make up your life as it is today. If you want to change the *effects*, you must change the *causes*. If you want to change what you are getting out, you must change what you are putting in.

This Law of Cause and Effect is the foundation law of Western thought. This law underlies and is the "granddaddy law" of mathematics, science, physics, medicine, technology, business, and warfare.

Natural laws, mental or physical, work 100 percent of the time. It does not matter whether you know about them, agree with them, like them, or whether they are particularly convenient for you at a particular time. They are *neutral*. They work for everyone, at all times, under all circumstances.

Our main job is to understand them and, especially for the mental laws, conform our behavior to them if we want them to act on our behalf. There are three main mental laws.

The Law of Belief

The first, the Law of Belief, is the foundation principle of all philosophy, religion, psychology, metaphysics, and success. According to this law, whatever you believe with *feeling*, with *emotion*, becomes your reality. Wayne Dyer says, "You don't believe what you see; you see what you have already decided to believe."

It doesn't even matter if your belief is true. If you believe it long enough and intensely enough, it becomes true for you, whether it is positive or negative.

BELIEFS ARE LEARNED

The interesting thing about beliefs is that no one is born with them. Everything that you believe today about yourself, other people, and the world you have learned from someone, somehow, at some time. Whatever the source, once you start to believe it, it becomes your truth because it is true for you.

Each person holds two types of beliefs: positive and negative. The very worst of these beliefs in terms of success are *self-limiting beliefs*. These are beliefs that you have about yourself or your business that limit you, that hold you back, and often undermine all of your hopes for success and achievement. What are yours?

Your negative or self-limiting beliefs are the brakes or barriers to your success, whether or not they are true. And the great discovery is that most of your self-limiting beliefs are *not true at all.* They are the result of something that someone has said to you, something you read or heard in a class or that you picked up along the way without giving it much thought.

CHALLENGE YOUR SELF-LIMITING BELIEFS

For you to achieve your full potential, you must eliminate the self-limiting beliefs that hold you back. For you to move on to the highway of personal progress and success, you must give up all beliefs that suggest that you may be limited with regard to your intelligence, your creativity, your natural ability, and your personality. You must be willing to give up any idea that may be holding you back from achieving your full potential.

The Law of Attraction

The second major mental law that determines what happens to you is the Law of Attraction. It states that you are a "living magnet," and that you inevitably attract into your life the people, events, and circumstances that are in harmony with your dominant thoughts, especially your dominant thoughts emotionalized.

Everything you have in your life today you have attracted to yourself by the person you are, by the way you think. You can change your life because you can change the person you are. You can change the thoughts that you think.

CHANGE YOUR THINKING, CHANGE YOUR LIFE

If you wish to attract different people, circumstances, opportunities, or a better job or higher income into your life, you have to change your thinking about yourself in that area.

There is a general success principle that says, "Your income will be the average income of the five people with whom you spend the most time."

Why? It is because we are inordinately influenced by the people around us. As much as 95 percent of the way we think and feel about ourselves and our world is determined by the people with whom we habitually associate.

I have worked with countless people who moved from a job working under a negative boss, with negative coworkers, to a company where they worked under a positive boss with positive coworkers. Within a few weeks, their work lives had transformed. They went from being average performers to being superstars. Their incomes often increased several times.

The Law of Correspondence

According to this third important mental law, your outer life is a mirror image of your inner life. Your external world reflects your internal world. As they say in Zen, "Everywhere you go, there you are."

You don't see the world the way it is. You see the world the way you are. This means that you can look around you at any time of your life at the people, circumstances, income, and environment and you will discover that they will always correspond to your inner life at that time.

When people are unhappy or dissatisfied with their outer life of work or relationships, it is quite common for them to begin to engage in negative behaviors, such as eating or drinking too much and exercising too little.

It is quite common for people who have entered into a new, happier relationship to start dieting, exercising, and taking much better care of their physical health.

THINK IT AND BE IT

One of the most important discoveries about the power of the human mind is that you become what you think about, most of the time.

What do you think about, most of the time? It is easy to tell. Whatever people think about, their mental equivalent, will always be manifested in their external circumstances. Just look at them and around them.

You must create the mental equivalent on the *inside* of what you want to see manifested on the *outside*. When you do this, you will dramatically improve the quality of your life. This will happen not because of luck or chance, but because of law—the Law of Cause and Effect.

ACTION EXERCISES

1. Identify a self-limiting belief that could be holding you back. Challenge it. Imagine that it is not true. What would you do then?

2. Think about your outer life—your work and your relationships. Are you happy with your life? If not, what are you going to do?

TWO

Decide Exactly What You Want

KNOWING WHAT you want is the starting point of personal progress and career success. You can have almost anything you want in life, but first you have to decide what it is.

H. L. Hunt, the oil billionaire and founder of more than 200 companies, was once asked on television what he thought to be the secret of success. He replied, "Success is simple. First, decide exactly what it is that you want in life. Most people never do this. Second, determine the price that you are going to have to pay to achieve it, and then resolve to pay that price."

Clarity Is Essential

In deciding exactly what you want, start with your values. What is it that you believe in and care about? You will only be successful on the outside if you are working toward those things that you consider valuable and important on the inside.

Identify Your Career Goals

Think about your career goals. Imagine you could wave a magic wand and project forward five years into the future. Where would you like to be in one, three, or five years? If your work life was perfect, what would it look like, and how would it be different from today?

Many people start their careers by taking the first job that is offered to them. From then on, they do what other people want, what other people ask them to do. They accept jobs that are offered to them, take promotions from their superiors, and continuously react and respond to the demands put upon them by others.

Successful people plan their careers carefully. They determine where they want to be at certain points in the future and the level of skills that they will need in particular areas to achieve that career goal.

Set Personal and Family Goals

The second type of goals that you need are personal and family goals. If your career and income goals are the "what" that you need to do, your personal family goals are the "why." These are the reasons you are doing what you are doing. These are the reasons you get up in the morning and go to work.

Fully 85 percent of your happiness will be determined by your relationships and the people in your life. Only 15 percent of your happiness or satisfaction will come from the things you achieve of a material nature. Whatever satisfaction you derive from material accomplishments will very quickly dissipate and disappear, like cigarette smoke in a large room.

Determine your personal goals as well. Think about the level of health and fitness that you would like to enjoy, if you had no limitations. What subjects would you like to learn about? What destinations would you like to visit? What contributions would you like to make to your community?

The Seven-Step Process

There is a simple seven-step process that you can use for setting and achieving your goals for the rest of your life. It is powerful, proven, and practical.

1. *Decide exactly what you want.* Be specific. Don't make the mistake of saying things like, "I want to be rich. I want to be happier. I want to be healthy. I want to travel." These are not goals. These are wishes, illusions, and fantasies. A goal is something that is clear and specific.

2. *Write it down.* Only 3 percent of adults have written goals with clear plans to accomplish them. These people earn, on average, ten times as much as people without written goals and plans.

3. *Set a deadline.* Determine a specific date for when you wish to achieve your goal. If it is a big enough goal, set sub-deadlines.

4. *Make a list.* Write down everything you can think of that you can possibly do to achieve your goal, and keep adding to the list until the list is complete.

5. *Organize the list.* Create a checklist of the things you need to do, and in the specific order that they need to be done. What do you need to do first? Second? Third? And so on. A list of activities organized into a checklist becomes a plan of action.

6. *Take action on your plan.* Do something. Do anything. But take action immediately. Taking the first step is the most difficult step. The hardest job, it's said, is the one on which you never get started.

7. *Do something every day on your most important goal.* Do something seven days a week, thirty days a month. Never let a day go by where you don't do something that moves you at least one step forward toward something that is important to you.

Select Ten Goals

Take a clean sheet of paper and at the top write the word *Goals* plus today's date. Then, write down ten goals that you would like to accomplish over the next twelve months. You can have goals for one day or one week, or for twelve months. But make sure all the goals are attainable within one year.

Once you have written out ten goals, ask yourself this question: If I could achieve any one goal on this list within twenty-four hours, which one goal would have the greatest positive impact on my life?

This, then, becomes your major definite purpose, your *focal point*, the organizing principle of your life. Napoleon Hill said people only begin to become great when they settle on their "definiteness of purpose."

Fully 85 percent of self-made millionaires have a single, burning goal that they work on every day. So should you.

Purposeful action is the starting point of all great success. The more you engage in systematic, planned action toward your predetermined goals and objectives, the more rapidly you accomplish the things you want.

ACTION EXERCISES

1. Make a list of ten goals that you would like to accomplish in the next twelve months.

2. Select the one goal that could have the greatest positive impact on your life, make a plan for its achievement, and work on it every single day until you are successful.

THREE

Develop the Habits of Courage and Self-Confidence

IN 3,300 STUDIES of leadership, reviewed by historian James McPherson, going back to 600 BC, the two most common qualities of leaders identified were *vision* and *courage*. First of all, have a clear vision or goal of your desired future, and second, have the courage to do whatever is necessary to achieve that goal or to realize that vision.

Winston Churchill said, "Courage is rightly considered the foremost of the virtues, for upon it, all others depend."

The development of courage and self-confidence is absolutely essential for success, because it is the fear of failure that holds back most people. In the *Forbes 400* listing of the richest people in America in 2015, the self-made billionaires listed "the willingness to take risks" as one of the five most important qualities to which they attributed their success.

Fears Can Be Unlearned

The fear of failure is *learned*, usually in early childhood, as a result of destructive criticism from parents and siblings. But because it is learned, it can also be unlearned and replaced with the habit of courage.

Remember that FEAR stands for False Experiences Appearing Real. The fear of failure is not based on reality, but on imagination. Fully 99 percent of the things we worry about never come to pass. Fear is a belief, and as William James of Harvard said, "Belief creates the actual fact."

Ralph Waldo Emerson gave us the antidote to fear. He said, "Do the thing you fear and the death of fear is certain." If you do the thing you fear, over and over again, eventually it loses all of its power.

Move Toward the Fear

What is the difference between the brave man or woman and the coward? The answer is that the brave person confronts the fear, moves toward the fear, deals with the fear, and resolves the fearful situation. The cowardly person, on the other hand, backs away from the fear, avoids the fear, and hopes that the fear will go away by itself.

When you move toward something that you fear, the fear diminishes in size and influence, becoming smaller and smaller, and eventually it has no influence over your emotions.

But if you back away from the fear or avoid the fear-inducing person or situation, it grows and grows and soon takes over your whole life. Everyone has had this experience.

Whenever you experience fear of any kind, you can cancel the fear by immediately saying those magic words, *I can do it! I can do it! I can do it!*

The truth is that you can do anything that you put your mind to, if only you want it hard enough. There are no real limits except the limits you place on your own thinking. It is only self-limiting beliefs, which are largely under your control, that hold you back.

Act As If . . .

One of the keys to developing courage and confidence is to "act as if" you already have the qualities of courage and confidence that you desire. Act as if the fear did not exist. Pretend that you are not afraid. Think about yourself as having no fear at all in whatever situation may be holding you back.

Act as if, and ask yourself, "How would I behave and act, walk and talk, if I had no fear at all?"

"Fake it until you make it." Pretend that you are not afraid and eventually your subconscious mind will accept that you are not afraid, and the fear will go away.

Make a habit of courage. Whenever you have a choice of backing up or going forward, always dare to go forward. There is a Zulu saying, "If you face two dangers, one behind you and one in front of you, always go forward toward the one in front of you." Keep making the decision to go forward until it becomes so automatic that you don't back away from anything.

Your Health and Happiness

Courage is absolutely essential to personal success and psychological health, and courage is a learned quality. Even if you have had experiences in the past that have caused you to be hesitant or fearful in certain situations, you can overcome this hesitancy and become as courageous as a linebacker, just by practicing courage over and over again.

A large percentage of successful people say that when they were young, during their formative years, they read biographies and autobiographies of successful men and women. They read the stories of people who had overcome obstacles and accomplished great things with their lives.

ACTION EXERCISES

1. Think of some person that you are nervous about confronting, or some action that you are afraid to take, and dare to go forward. Confront the fear. Deal with it and put it behind you.

2. Practice autosuggestion. Speak positively to yourself every day. Say the words, "I can do it! I can do anything I put my mind to," until it becomes your new reality.

FOUR

Be True to Yourself

YOUR REPUTATION is your most valuable asset. It is the way people think about you and talk about you that determines your success and advancement more than any other single factor. When people consider you to be a person of character, as well as competence, your future is assured.

Peter Drucker said that "integrity is the most important quality of leadership." It is how much people believe you and trust you and know that you will do what you say you will do that is more important than any other factor.

Make it a habit to practice honesty and integrity in everything you do. Without integrity, nothing else is possible. Lack of integrity in a single area is often the fatal flaw that holds people back for their entire lives.

Integrity Defined

In defining integrity, we are not talking about cheating, lying, and robbing other people. Most people don't do these things. Ninety percent of people are usually quite honest.

Integrity means being true to yourself, being perfectly honest with yourself in all respects. This is where real integrity begins. If you are not honest with yourself, you will have a tendency to be dishonest with other people. The key is to speak the truth, and then live in truth with everyone.

Shakespeare said, "And this above all: to thine own self be true, and it must follow, as the night the day, thou canst not then be false to any man."

Your Innermost Values

Being honest with yourself means that you live consistent with your innermost values and convictions. You only do work that you care about, that you feel is important, and that makes a difference in the lives of other people.

Perhaps the most important word is *caring*. If you really care about your work, it's probably the work that you were meant to do. If you don't care about your work, you would be in effect living a lie. If you do not feel fully engaged with your work, it doesn't mean that there is something wrong with your job. It is just that this job is wrong for *you*. And you will never be successful doing something that you don't care about.

Trust Your Intuition

Ralph Waldo Emerson said, "Trust yourself: every heart vibrates to that iron string." Listen to what is called the "still, small voice" within you. The starting point of true greatness in human life is when you begin listening to that voice, when you begin trusting your intuition and going with the flow of what it tells you to do.

Earl Nightingale said, "When you begin listening to your inner voice, you will probably never make another mistake."

The wonderful thing about your intuition is that it is always right, always true. Whenever you are unsure of what to do, take a few moments in solitude and just listen. Your inner voice will almost always give you the exact direction that you need and tell you your correct course of action.

At the same time, resolve to never do anything that is inconsistent with that little voice. When you follow the guidance of your inner voice, you'll seldom be wrong. And the more you trust this little voice, the more accurate it becomes and the faster it functions.

Keep Your Promises

Always keep your promises. Give promises sparingly, but once you have committed to doing something, resolve to follow through, no matter how much it costs.

There is an interesting point about promises. Whenever you make a promise and then keep that promise, especially when there is an unexpected effort or sacrifice involved, you feel better about yourself. Your self-esteem and self-confidence increase. Keeping your promises makes you feel stronger inside. It gives you higher levels of self-respect and personal pride.

But whenever you break a promise, or fail to follow through on a promise that you have made, it makes you feel negative and inferior inside. It makes you feel weak and small. Not fulfilling your promises often causes you to criticize, complain, and condemn others. You make excuses like, "Everybody does it."

Be a Person of Honor

There are two types of promises. There are the promises that you make to others and the promises that you make to *yourself.* Just as it is important for your reputation to keep your word and to be known as a person of honor in your relationships with others, it is also vital that you keep your promises to yourself.

If you promise yourself that you are going to exercise each day, improve your diet, be punctual for meetings, or complete a course of study, it is essential that you keep these promises. Even though no one else may know about your promises, when you make a promise to yourself and you fail to fulfill your promise, it undermines your self-confidence and self-esteem.

Promise slowly. Promise carefully. Promise thoughtfully, but once you make a promise to yourself or anyone else, discipline yourself to carry it out. You will be amazed at the difference in the way people see you and the way you feel about yourself.

ACTION EXERCISES

1. Identify one area in your life where you do not feel comfortable or committed, and resolve to either get in fully or to get out completely.

2. Identify promises that you have made to others or to yourself that you have not yet kept, and resolve to fulfill those promises by a specific date.

FIVE

Develop a Positive Mental Attitude

SHAKESPEARE WROTE, "Nothing is either good or bad, but thinking makes it so."

There is a formula that says that it is your *attitude* more than your *aptitude* that determines your *altitude*.

The more positive and constructive you become, the more you will be liked and respected. You will be paid more and promoted faster. More people will like you, support you, want to be around you, and cooperate with you.

The more positive you become, the more influential and persuasive you will be with other people. Like flowers opening up in the sunshine, people open up to those who are warm and friendly toward them.

Maya Angelou famously said, "People will forget what you do and say, but they will always remember how you made them feel."

Learned Optimism

Fully 85 percent of your success and advancement is going to be determined by your attitude. According to Martin Seligman of the University of Pennsylvania, the most important quality to predict success and happiness in life is *optimism*. And optimism is a quality that not only can be measured, but can also be learned.

How do you learn to become an optimist—a completely positive person? Well, since you become what you think about most of the time, the key to becoming an optimist is for you to think the way optimists think until it becomes second nature. And how do optimists think, most of the time?

THINK ABOUT WHAT YOU WANT

Optimists think about what they want and how to get it. They think about their goals and the specific steps that they can take each day and each hour to move themselves in the direction of their goals. Each step you take toward a goal that is important to you makes you feel positive, powerful, and more optimistic.

Here is an important point. Your conscious mind can hold hundreds of thoughts in a row, but it can only hold one thought at a time, either positive or negative. If you deliberately fill your mind with a positive thought about a goal you want to achieve and the specific actions you can take to achieve it, you automatically block out negative thoughts.

One of the greatest of all success principles is for you to think about your goals all the time—morning, noon, and night. Whenever you have a negative experience, think about your goal. Whenever you have a setback or disappointment, think about your goal. Use the thinking about your goal to cancel out the negatives until it becomes automatic and easy.

SEEK THE VALUABLE LESSON

Look for the valuable lesson in every setback or difficulty. Every problem or obstacle you have contains a *lesson* of some kind, and often several lessons. While you're looking for the lesson, asking what can be learned from this situation, your mind remains positive and you remain in complete control of your emotions.

FEED YOUR MIND CONTINUALLY

Feed your mind continually with positive ideas and information. Read positive books and articles, information that helps you and improves your life and work. Listen to positive, educational audio programs on your smartphone, in your car, and whenever else you have a chance. Attend positive talks, seminars, and workshops where you learn valuable, constructive ideas that you can use to improve the quality of your life.

CONTROL YOUR ATTITUDE

Your attitude is composed of two parts: your attitude toward *yourself* and your attitude toward *others*. The more you think of yourself as a valuable, good, and worthwhile person, the more optimistic, positive, and successful you will be.

The more you have a positive attitude toward yourself, the more you will have a positive attitude toward others as well. The two are interrelated. There seems to be a one-to-one relationship between the two types of attitude.

You Need Other People

Everything you ever achieve in your work will require the help and cooperation of other people, often lots of people. Today, people will only help you if they want to, not because they have to. When you are consistently positive toward others, looking for the good, listening sympathetically, asking lots of questions, people will warm up to you and become open to your influence. They will want to help you, work with you, and cooperate with you to help you achieve your goals.

The Carnegie Institute of Technology did a study some years ago and found that 95 percent of people who had been fired from large companies over a ten-year period were let go because of an inability to get along well with others. It was their negative attitude and not their lack of competence.

People with positive attitudes always tend to be promoted and moved into positions of greater responsibility. This is because those people in a position to control their advancement prefer to be around nice people.

ACTION EXERCISES

1. Think about your goals and the steps you can take each day and each hour to achieve those goals. Continuously fill your mind with positive thoughts about the goals you want to achieve until you become a genuinely positive person.

2. Identify one of the lessons that you can learn from a difficult situation you are dealing with today. Look into the lesson for something valuable that can help you be even more successful in the future.

SIX

Communicate Positively and Expect the Best

HOW YOU communicate largely determines the quality of your life. In a study, senior executives were asked to name the most important skills in leadership and in business. Eighty-six percent said that the ability to communicate was the key skill, more important than all others.

This ability to communicate includes not only communication with others, but also how you communicate with *yourself* in terms of your inner dialogue and positive self-talk.

Your Explanatory Style

Fully 95 percent of your emotions are determined by your inner dialogue or "explanatory style." When you explain things to yourself and others in a positive, constructive way, you remain calm, clear, and in control of the situation. If you explain or interpret things in a negative way, you immediately become negative, angry, and less effective.

Choose your words carefully. Use positive words rather than negative words. Instead of using the word *problem*, which is a negative word that triggers negative emotions, use the word *situation*, which is a neutral word.

Even better, use the word *challenge*. Say, "We are facing an interesting challenge here today," or an unexpected challenge, or an unusual challenge.

A challenge is something that you rise to—something that brings out the very best in you and in others. It is actually something that you look forward to in a positive way.

The best word of all to use to describe a problem is the word *opportunity*. Some of the biggest opportunities in business and in life initially come disguised as problems, obstacles, or even complete failures of a product or a career.

POSITIVE SELF-TALK

Always speak positively about yourself. Be careful never to say anything about yourself that you do not want to be true. Never criticize yourself or put yourself down. If you make a mistake, immediately cancel it by saying something like, "Next time I'll do better."

When people ask you how things are going, you tell them everything is going great. Even if you are having problems, you don't need to voice your concerns or share your problems with others.

PROGRAM YOUR SUBCONSCIOUS

When you speak positively to yourself about yourself, these words are soon accepted by your subconscious mind as commands. Your subconscious mind will then actualize feelings, body language, and emotions that are consistent with your self-talk. Speak to yourself the way that you want to be, not the way you may be today. The more you do this, the more you will feel the emotions that are consistent with your words.

Remain optimistic and cheerful on the outside. Be a constant voice of encouragement and reinforcement to the people around you. Tell your staff that they are doing a good job. Thank them on a regular basis for small and large accomplishments.

Positive Expectations

One of the most powerful motivational tools of all is maintaining positive expectations, both of yourself and others. This is why you look for the good in people and in every situation.

The effect of positive expectations has been researched for many years at Harvard University by David Rosenthal. What he found was that we tend to get not what we want, but what we expect in life.

Not only that, but your expectations, spoken or unspoken, have a powerful effect on the behavior of other people.

When you are growing up, the expectations your parents had for you had an inordinate impact on the person you became and your beliefs about yourself as an adult. Most problems in adult life can be traced back to criticism and negative expectations experienced in the first three to five years of life.

YOUR EXPECTATIONS AFFECT YOUR LIFE

Your expectations of your *spouse* and *children* have an inordinate impact on how they turn out and how they feel about themselves. Always tell them that you expect the very best from them in whatever they do.

The expectations of your *boss* have a direct influence on your performance and how you feel about your work. The very best bosses are known as "positive expectations bosses." They are always expressing a high level of confidence in the people that report to them.

Your expectations of your *staff* influence them as well. The rule is always to look for the good in each person and expect the best. You will seldom be disappointed.

Finally, your expectations of *yourself* are the most influential of all. If you expect to do well, you will do well. If you expect to be successful, you will be successful. If you expect to follow through with your diet or your learning plan, you will probably do it.

EXPECT GREAT THINGS

When you expect great things from yourself and the people around you, you'll seldom be disappointed. But if you expect negative things, you will seldom be disappointed there, either.

W. Clement Stone, one of the richest men in America in his time, having started as an orphan delivering papers on the streets of Chicago, urged each person to become an "inverse paranoid."

A paranoid is a person who is convinced that the world is conspiring to hurt him in some way. Paranoids are distrustful and suspicious of others. They expect the worst in almost every situation. They are constantly looking over their shoulder, convinced that others are "out to get them."

An *inverse* paranoid, on the other hand, is a person who is convinced that the world is conspiring to do good, to help the person be more successful. Inverse paranoids look upon every person, problem, and situation as part of a large conspiracy that has been organized to help them be more successful in the future.

Communicate positively with yourself. Communicate positively with others. Always expect the best. Always look for the good. Always tell people how much you appreciate and believe in them. You will be amazed at the difference this outlook will make in your career.

ACTION EXERCISES

1. Get up each morning and say emphatically, "I feel happy! I feel healthy! I feel terrific!" Throughout the day, whenever anybody asks you how you are feeling, reply with a big smile and say, "I feel terrific!"

2. Always expect the best of yourself and others. Tell others that you have complete confidence that they are going to be successful or do a great job. Your expectations will shape both their emotions and their behaviors.

SEVEN

Develop a Bias for Action

OVER THE YEARS, I have done more than 5,000 interviews on radio and TV, in magazines, newsletters, newspapers, blogs, and in front of audiences. Over and over, people ask me, "What is the secret of success?"

But, as Og Mandino once told me, "There are no secrets of success; there are merely timeless truths that have been discovered over and over again."

That being said, I think that one of the great secrets of success in business is simply "task completion." In the final analysis, you will be judged by your ability to get results that people want, need, value, and will pay you for. People who are paid high salaries and get promoted to senior positions are people who have developed a reputation for getting the job done—for getting results far in excess of those achieved by the average employee.

Focus on Results

Peter Drucker said that the first question of an executive should be, "What results are expected of me?" This should be your first question as well.

The key to task completion is simply to "get going and keep going." David Allen's popular time management book is called *Getting Things Done*. That really summarizes the beginning and end of accomplishment in the world of work.

In a study of 104 CEOs, respondents were asked what would be the most important qualities to advance in their organizations. Most of them agreed on two qualities. The first was the ability to set priorities: to determine what was more important and what was less important. The second quality for advancement was the ability to get started and then to get the job done quickly and well.

Move Quickly on Opportunities

Nothing will advance your career faster than your becoming known as the go-to guy or gal in your organization. The best reputation to develop is being the kind of person that others come to if they want something done quickly. If you want something done *eventually*, you give it to someone else. But whenever speed is of the essence, you are the person that they think of first.

A bias for action—a sense of urgency—is one of the most important qualities for promotion. Even if you have a reputation for doing excellent work, but you get it done slowly, that alone can hold you back more than you can imagine.

Action Orientation

Successful people have a series of "orientations," habitual ways of thinking that set them apart from the average. One of these is "action orientation." This is a bias for action that makes them think continuously about specific actions that they can take to achieve their goals and get the job done quickly.

They are constantly in motion. They walk quickly, move quickly, act quickly, think quickly, and even speak quickly. They are impatient. They think continually about starting and completing tasks.

If task completion is the key to success, and getting started on your tasks is the key to completing them, the next question is, "Which specific task should you work on?"

Do the Most Important First

The answer is simple. If you are going to work hard and fast, and do a quick and dependable job on a task, make sure that it is the most important single task that you can be working on in terms of the results that you are expected to get in your job.

Set priorities, determine the most important task, and then concentrate on it single-mindedly, 100 percent, until it's finished.

You want to earn more money? You want to get better and more valuable results—especially the results that your boss considers to be the most important results of all? Then determine the most important tasks that you can complete to make the greatest contribution to your organization, start on them, and work on them unceasingly until they are complete.

When you develop a bias for action and a sense of urgency to get started and keep going toward the completion of your major task, you put yourself automatically onto the fast track to success.

ACTION EXERCISES

1. Talk to your boss and determine the most important results that you can get in your work. Remember, working on anything other than your most important task is a relative waste of time. In fact, working on low-value tasks when you could be working on high-value tasks can actually sabotage your career.

2. Select one task—the most important task—start on it immediately, and then discipline yourself to work on it single-mindedly until it is complete. Repeat, over and over again, on all your top tasks until task completion becomes a habit.

EIGHT

Satisfy Your Most Important Customers

ALBERT EINSTEIN was once asked, "What is the purpose of human life?"

He pondered this question for a while and then replied, "We must be here to serve others. What other purpose could there be?"

We are here to serve others, in some way. This is true in our work just as it is true in our personal and family lives. In business, your rewards will always be in direct proportion to the value of your service to other people. If you want to increase your rewards, both financial and in terms of promotion, you must focus on increasing the value of your service.

Identify Your Customers

Who are your customers? This is one of the most important questions you ever ask and answer. Your customers are the people upon whom you are dependent for your advancement, and the people who are dependent upon you for something that they need and want.

With this definition, you have *three* main customers: your boss, your subordinates, and the customers for the products and services that you produce.

Your Boss

Your boss is your main customer. Your success and happiness in your career is going to be largely if not totally determined by how much you please your boss and how positive your boss feels toward you.

Some people miss this point completely. They think that they work for the company, and they see their boss in either a neutral or a critical way. They don't realize that their entire future will be determined by how happy they make their main customer, their boss, every single day.

MY BIG BREAK

One day, I received a phone call from a powerful executive, the president and owner of one of the biggest companies in the country. I had met and spoken with him a couple of times, so he was aware of my existence. He asked me if I would like to come to work for him as his personal assistant. I immediately accepted.

From then on, not knowing much about the way corporations worked, I focused on one thing. I did whatever he asked me to do, and I did it quickly and well, and it turned out to be enough.

He guided and instructed me like a sports coach. He told me what to do more of and what to do less of. I met with him almost every evening for an hour to get his guidance and instruction. Within a year, I was running three divisions of the company and I was responsible for generating millions of dollars of revenue. I had three offices, each with their own staff. He moved me up the ladder faster than anyone who had ever worked for him in his more than 200 companies and his thirty-year business career.

THE SIMPLE SECRET

My secret was simple. I recognized that he was my primary customer. As long as I made him happy, I was completely free of the politics and backbiting that take place in a large corporation.

In no time, I became the "go-to guy" in that company. When important assignments came up, he called me in first and handed them to me. It was my job to figure out how to do the work and to hire the more than thirty people I eventually needed.

Your Staff and Coworkers

Your second set of customers are your staff and coworkers. These are people you depend on, and who depend on you. The very best companies and work teams have the most open communications. Everyone knows what everyone else is doing and how each person's job fits into the bigger picture. There is active, ongoing discussion about the work and how each person can make a more valuable contribution to getting the results the department or company expects.

Your Customer or Client

Your third customer is, of course, the one who purchases the products and services that your company produces. This is the most important customer of all, which is why Tom Peters said that the most important principle for success in business is "an obsession with customer service."

Who are your most important customers? What do they consider value? Why do they buy your products or services? What can you do to serve them, satisfy them, and please them, and make them happier than your competitors?

The Key to Business Success

Sometimes people ask me what I think is the key to business success. I tell them that all of business success can be summarized in two letters: ER. To be successful in business, you have to make your customers happy. Everyone knows that. But to be really successful, you have to make them happier. You have to serve them fast*er*, bett*er*, cheap*er*, and make it easi*er* for them to do business with you than with anyone else.

In the same way, your success is determined by those two letters. What can you do, starting today, to please your most important customers bett*er* than anyone else? What can you do to make them happi*er*? In your ability to ask, answer, and deliver on this question lies your future.

ACTION EXERCISES

1. Who are your most important customers, the ones you most depend on for your success and who depend on you for their success and satisfaction?

2. Decide on at least one thing that you can do immediately to make your most important customer happier with your work and service than with that of anyone else.

NINE

Be a Hard Worker

WHEN I WAS a teenager, I had a quite common ambition—to be a millionaire by the time I was thirty. By the time I was thirty, I was still broke and struggling. When I was thirty-five, I began giving seminars and workshops on personal and business success. One day, the president of a national corporation with more than 800 branches, all independently owned, asked me if I would speak at the company's annual meeting on the subject of how to become a self-made millionaire.

Of course, I agreed. Beginning speakers will engage almost any audience on almost any subject. But when I hung up the phone, I realized that even though becoming a self-made millionaire had been my ambition for my whole adult life, I didn't know very much about self-made millionaires. This changed my life.

What I Learned

Fortunately, I had two months to prepare for this seminar. I immediately went to work and began researching every source I could find about self-made millionaires. I was astonished to find that there was an enormous body of research on this subject. Over the years, thousands of self-made millionaire had been interviewed and asked the question, "How did you start with nothing and become a millionaire in one generation?"

Thomas Stanley, coauthor with William Danko of the bestseller *The Millionaire Next Door*, conducted several years of what was probably the best research ever done on self-made millionaires. Their finding: Fully 85 percent of self-made millionaires said that the key to their success was *hard, hard work*. They said things like, "I didn't get great grades in school. I didn't come from a wealthy family. I was not as smart or talented as other people. But I had one thing. I was willing to work harder than anyone else."

The Common Denominator

It seems that hard work is the common denominator of self-made millionaires, billionaires, and high achievers in every field. There is probably nothing that will bring you to the attention of your superiors faster than a reputation for working harder than anyone else. This requires that you start a little earlier, work a little harder, and stay a little later. High achievers always do more than is expected of them. They put in more time than anyone else puts in. They don't do only what they've been asked to do; they do a little bit more. It's that little bit more that makes all the difference.

Go the extra mile. No one can stop you from doing more than you are paid for. And if you do more than you are being paid for today, you will eventually be paid far more than you are receiving today. And remember, there are never any traffic jams on the extra mile.

All Things Are *Not* Equal

There is a good deal of talk and political controversy around the subject of "inequality" in our society. Why is it that some people and families earn far more than other people and families? The reasons are not pleasing to many people.

The answer is quite simple. Successful people and families work far more hours than unsuccessful people and families. People in the top 20 percent of income in America work an average of sixty hours per week. People and families in the bottom 20 percent of income work less than twenty hours a week, and some of them don't work at all.

Not only that, people in the top 20 percent work much harder during those many more hours that they put in. People in the bottom 20 percent usually do the very minimum possible to avoid losing their jobs.

Self-made millionaires work an average of fifty-nine hours a week, and often seventy and eighty hours, for many years. David Foster, the music impresario, was once asked what he did on the weekends to relax. He paused to think about his answer and then said, "I don't know any successful people who work less than six days a week."

Work All the Time You Work

Here's another key to success: Work all the time you work. When you go to work, don't waste time. Put your head down and work flat out all day. If someone wants to talk to you, say, "I would love to talk, but right now I have to get *back to work*. Why don't we talk afterward?"

According to Robert Half & Associates, 50 percent of working time is wasted, mostly in idle chitchat with coworkers and playing on the Internet and social networking sites. The average employee comes in at the last minute, takes longer coffee breaks and lunches, sometimes goes shopping during the day, takes care of personal business, reads the paper, and leaves at the first possible minute.

The above description does not apply to high performers and people on the fast track. They plan their work and they work their plan. They come in and start work like a runner, taking off when the gun is fired. They work all day and they don't waste time. They work on high-priority items. They work on those tasks that are most important to their bosses and to their companies. Everyone knows who the hard workers are in every organization. And everyone knows who the slackers are as well.

The Harder You Work, The Better You Get

Here is an exercise for you: Imagine that they are going to do a secret survey to determine who the hardest-working person in your company might be. No one else but you knows that this research study is being conducted. Make it your goal to win this contest. Make a decision that, at the end of the year, everyone in your company will vote for you as the hardest-working employee.

The good news is that the harder you work, the better you get. The better you get, the more and better work you can do. The more and better work you do, the faster you get promoted and the more you get paid. When you develop a reputation for being the hardest worker in your business, a whole new world opens up for you.

ACTION EXERCISES

1. From now on, resolve to start work one hour earlier each day. Throughout the day, work all the time you work, and resolve to work one hour later than everyone else. This will double your productivity, performance, and output from the very first day.

2. Select the most important task you can accomplish and start on it first thing each morning, working at it single-mindedly until it is completed each day.

TEN

Dedicate Yourself to Continuous Learning

EVERYONE WANTS to be paid more and promoted faster. But most people hope that it happens by a process of osmosis. They actually think that their income prospects are determined by their bosses and by economic forces.

But we determine our own income by what we do and what we fail to do. We are where we are and what we are because we have *decided* to be there, either consciously or unconsciously. If you are not happy with your current income, go to the nearest mirror and negotiate with your boss. That is the person who determines how much you earn.

You Are Maxed Out Today
The truth is that you have maxed out your income today at your current level of knowledge and skill. You have gone as

far as you can go with what you already know. If you want to earn more in the future, you must take in new knowledge and develop new skills that will enable you to get more and better results that other people want, need, and are willing to pay for.

The good news is that you can become anything you want to be if you are willing to study hard enough and prepare yourself for it. Continuous self-improvement means the continuous upgrading of your skills, constant training, continuous learning, and always moving ahead.

The 80/20 Rule Again

Gary Becker, the late Nobel Prize–winning economist from the University of Chicago, conducted a study on income inequality. What he found was that the population falls into roughly two categories, the top 20 percent and the bottom 80 percent.

Becker discovered that people in the bottom 80 percent increased their income at about 3 percent per annum, which is one percent above the rate of inflation. As such, they never get ahead. They are always in debt. They worry about money all their lives. And when they reach retirement age they have very little set aside for the years ahead.

Becker also found that the people in the bottom 80 percent very seldom learned anything new after they took their first job. They did the same job in the same way, year after year, never reading, learning, studying, or upgrading their skills. Because they were surrounded by other people who were also not learning anything new and not going anywhere in their careers, they automatically assumed that this lifestyle of nonlearning was the way everyone lived.

The Top Earners

But Becker also found that the top 20 percent of income earners increased their income at an average of about 11 percent per year. The reason was simple. They were continuous lifelong learners.

The top 20 percent of income earners were those people who read all the business and personal development books. They attended all the seminars and workshops to advance their skills. They bought and listened to all the educational programs they could find. They continually associated with other people of like mind. Their most common form of conversation was ideas, insights, and sources of new information that they could use to become more productive and get better results, faster and easier.

The Three-Part Formula

There are three ways that you can become a continuous learner for the rest of your life. When you practice these three ideas, your life will change, and sometimes faster than you could imagine. One new idea or insight that applies to your work can advance your career by one, two, and even five years.

READ EVERY DAY

First, resolve to read at least *one hour* each day in your field. Put aside the newspapers and magazines, shut off the television, turn off your computer, and concentrate on reading something valuable and helpful to your career.

If you read the best business books in your field one hour a day, you will read an average of one book a week. One book per week translates into fifty books a year. Since it takes the reading and synthesizing of thirty to fifty books to get a PhD from a leading university, you can earn the equivalent of a doctorate in your field each year by simply reading one hour a day, and then thinking about how to apply your new ideas to getting better results.

LISTEN AND LEARN

Second, listen to audio learning programs at every opportunity. Listen to CDs in your car. Listen to the best audio books on your smartphone when you are driving, walking, flying, or waiting at the airport.

On average, people spend 500 to 1,000 hours in their car every year. That is the equivalent of twelve to twenty-four workweeks (of forty hours a week). This is the equivalent of one or two university semesters.

GO BACK TO SCHOOL

Third, take all the training you can get. Take seminars offered by your company or outside your company. Pay for additional training yourself if you have to.

Once you've determined your career path, figure out what you need to learn to get to where you're going. Become an expert on time management and personal communications. Become an expert on goal setting, problem solving, decision making, and strategic planning. Learn the skills that you need to learn to move ahead faster.

ACTION EXERCISES

1. Ask yourself this question: What one skill, if you were absolutely excellent at it, would help you the most to move ahead faster in your career?

   Whatever your answer, make a plan to learn this skill and work on it every single day. Remember, to achieve a goal (income) that you've never achieved before, you have to learn and practice a skill that you've never had before.

2. Commit to lifelong learning. Read a little bit every day. Listen to audio programs as you travel to and from work. Attend courses and seminars. Become a sponge for new information, constantly seeking those gems of ideas that can help you the most to move ahead in your career.

ELEVEN

Become a Competent Speaker

DEVELOPING THE ability to speak on your feet can accelerate your career by five or ten years. The ability to speak in public will contribute enormously to your overall confidence, poise, courage, and self-assurance. Learning to speak is an investment that pays off for life. And you can learn it if you want to learn it.

People who can speak in front of audiences are considered to be more knowledgeable, more intelligent, more competent, and more influential than others. When you stand up and speak persuasively, you are seen as being better informed and more articulate and having greater conviction than people who cannot speak in public.

Overcome the Fear

According to the Guinness World Records, the fear of public speaking is greater than the fear of death. A majority of adults (54 percent) rank public speaking as the worst of all possible experiences. Even the thought of having to speak in public can cause most people's stomachs to churn and their hearts to beat faster. The thought alone makes them shake and tremble.

Fortunately, everyone has the ability to speak competently and confidently in front of others. In fact, in my speaking seminars I like to say, "Everyone in this room started off as an excellent public speaker. You made your first public speech stark naked in front of a room full of strangers immediately after you were born."

Fear of public speaking is a learned fear. No one is born with it. People develop this fear over the course of a lifetime as the result of negative experiences that are reinforced. They then develop the self-limiting belief that "that's just the way I am." But it's not true.

Speaking Is a Learnable Skill

Competence in public speaking and making business presentations is a skill set—habits that you can learn with practice and repetition.

Elbert Hubbard, one of the most prolific writers in American history, was once asked how a person could become an excellent writer. He replied with these immortal words: "The only way to learn to write is to write and write and write and write and write and write."

To paraphrase Hubbard, the only way to learn to speak is to *speak and speak and speak and speak and speak and speak.*

By practicing speaking in front of small and large groups, your fear eventually disappears, to be replaced with feelings of confidence, courage, and excitement.

Get Started

Countless businesspeople have asked me how they can learn to speak competently. I give them the same answer. Join a local chapter of Toastmasters International and attend the weekly meetings. Alternately, call your local Dale Carnegie Training office and take a course in public speaking. Either one will do.

Both organizations use what psychologists call the process of "systematic desensitization." This means that they structure their meetings so that you get a chance to speak every time, over and over, until you eventually become more preoccupied with the preparation than with the speaking itself.

You Get Better and Better

The only way to learn to speak is by speaking. Having been in the professional speaking industry for more than thirty years, I have found there is a direct relationship between the number of times that a person has stood up and spoken in front of a group and how competent the person becomes in addressing an audience.

There is another benefit to learning how to speak in public, aside from the fact that you will give better presentations, sell more of your products, earn more money, and create a better life for yourself and your family. It greatly improves your self-confidence.

Short-Circuit the Fear

It seems that there is a direct relationship between the fear of rejection (hypersensitivity to the opinions and reactions of others) and the fear of public speaking. The two of them are wired together on the same circuit in the subconscious mind.

When you overcome the fear of public speaking, by continuous repetition, you simultaneously overcome the fear of rejection. As the fear of rejection declines, your self-confidence in approaching and dealing with other people increases. Salespeople who overcome their fear of rejection and their call reluctance (the anticipation that the prospect will be negative or uninterested in their product or service) soon find themselves absolutely unafraid of making more calls on more people.

One More Advantage

When you make a decision to overcome your fear of public speaking and you then follow through on your decision and become fearless speaking in front of an audience, for the rest of your life you will be *unafraid*. You will know from your own experience that you can confront and deal with whatever fear is holding you back and eliminate it forever. This is one of the most liberating of all experiences.

ACTION EXERCISES

1. Make a decision today to become an excellent public speaker over the next six to twelve months, and take action immediately.

2. Resolve to attend your first Toastmasters meeting within seven days. There are Toastmasters clubs in every community in America and worldwide. They are open to everyone.

TWELVE

Associate with the Right People

YOUR CHOICE of a peer group will determine as much as 95 percent of what you become in life. David McClelland of Harvard University spent many years researching why some people succeed and others don't, even when they have the same background, training, and opportunities. He found that it was the choice of the people you associate with on a day-to-day basis—your "reference group"—that as much as anything else determines your success or your failure.

McClelland found that the major factor that determined a positive change in your life was when you began to identify with a different type of person. His discovery was that when people were taken to a "place away"—a seminar, workshop, retreat, or some other location where they met, spoke with, and worked with a different type of person—they began to develop a new reference group. They began to think of themselves as more like *these* people than like the people back home.

Fly with the Eagles

Zig Ziglar, the motivational speaker, said it very well: "You can't fly with the eagles if you continue to scratch with the turkeys."

By getting away from negative people and instead associating with positive people, you begin to change the way you think, feel, and act. At an unconscious level, you start to ask yourself the question, "What would people like me, my new reference group, do in a situation like this?"

The Mastermind Concept

It is estimated that your average annual income will be the average income of the five people with whom you associate the most.

In Napoleon Hill's masterwork, *Think and Grow Rich*, he identified seventeen qualities of the richest self-made multimillionaires in America. The most important of these qualities, he said later in life, was the "mastermind concept." He observed that these top executives only began to move upward and onward rapidly when they began to associate on a regular basis with other top people.

You can form your own masterminds by identifying three or four people in your community you admire and want to be like. Call them or visit them personally and invite them to join you in a weekly mastermind session, either a breakfast or a lunch at a local café or restaurant.

You will be amazed at how quickly people agree to join a mastermind, if you invite them. At these meetings, you can use either a structured or an unstructured approach. You can simply let the conversation develop, moving from person to person and subject to subject for an hour, or you can have a specific focus for each meeting.

EVERYONE SUCCEEDS AT A HIGHER LEVEL

One of the most successful masterminds I ever saw was put together by a successful dermatologist. He invited a small group of people who were committed to personal and professional development to meet with him once a week at 6:30 a.m. in his office. The meetings went on until 8:00 a.m. when everyone left for work.

Prior to each meeting, they would agree on a book that everyone should read in the following week. At the next meeting, one person would be assigned the task of reviewing the book and telling the other members what he thought were the most important things he had learned from reading it. Then, they would go around the room and each other person would contribute ideas, comments, and experiences with regard to the book and its contents.

THE MASTERMIND EXPANDS

Eventually the group grew to about sixteen businesspeople, almost all of whom were in different occupations from each other. What I noticed, in following this group over a couple of years, was that the careers of every member took off after joining this group. Their incomes doubled and tripled. Their companies grew and flourished. They were promoted into senior positions. And they all attributed their new levels of success to their participation in this mastermind group.

Be Selective

Surround yourself with positive, goal-oriented people who are ambitious and excited about accomplishing wonderful things with their lives. It may be harsh, but don't spend time with people who are of no use to you. Baron de Rothschild once said, "Make no useless acquaintances." Avoid people who hold you back. Don't spend time in useless socializing with shallow people who have nothing to contribute. This is a major reason why people fail in life, and they don't even know it.

Everything counts! If you associate with people who cannot help you or benefit you in some way, then you are simultaneously deciding *not* to spend time with people who can help you. It is one or the other.

ACTION EXERCISES

1. Make a list of the people you associate with most of the time. Would you like to be like these people sometime in the future? Would you like your children to be like these people when they grow up? Does spending time with them enrich your life or not?

2. Form a mastermind group immediately. Invite two or three people who you like and admire to join you once a week, at breakfast or lunch, to talk about life, work, and the future. You will be amazed at what comes out of these meetings and what you learn.

THIRTEEN

Network Continually

ONE OF THE most important ways to advance your life and career is for you to network continually with other people in your field. Over the years, I have participated in more than a thousand meetings of organizations and associations. What has always interested me was the discovery that the top people always attend these meetings. The average or mediocre people always have a reason or an excuse not to attend.

There is an important rule for success. Your success will be in direct proportion to the number of people you know and who know you in a positive way. Put another way: "It is not what you know; it is who you know that determines your future.

Creative Job Search

When I developed a program on "Creative Job Search: How to Get and Keep the Job You Want in Any Economy," I was amazed to discover that 85 percent of new hires are made as the result of someone who knows someone else, and who then recommends that person for a job that was never advertised.

Sometimes, just knowing one person at the right time and place in your career can jump you ahead five years in terms of your income and position. But you never know who that person will be, so you have to meet lots and lots of people. And how do you do it? Networking!

Fish Where the Fish Are

How and where do you network? Simple. You fish where the fish are. You go to those places where the most important people, those who can help you the most and who you can help the most, can be found.

First of all, join one or two business associations in your community or nationally. Definitely join the national association for your industry or career. Look for the local chapters of your association, if they exist. If not, join general business associations such as the chamber of commerce. If you are a small businessperson, join your local Rotary, Lions, or Kiwanis chapter. If you are in sales, definitely join BNI—Business Network International. Each of these groups is full of people you need to know. These are people who you can help and who, in turn, can help you.

Be a Go-Giver

Many people think that networking consists of attending meetings, handing out your business card, and hustling for business. But nothing could be further from the truth. The very best networkers practice a simple strategy that works every single time.

When you meet new people, you have a singular focus: Determine what it is that you can do for them that will help them in their business. Forget about yourself. Be a "go-giver," rather than a "go-getter."

Ask open-ended questions and listen closely to the answers. People love to talk about themselves and their careers. Ask a lot of questions.

The more you ask questions of a person, and listen closely to the answers, nodding and smiling, the more the person likes you, respects you, and thinks that you are an intelligent and insightful individual.

One of the best questions that you can ask a businessperson is this: "What would I have to know about your product/service to recommend a new customer to you? Who are the best customers for what you sell?"

There is nothing that builds a stronger and faster bond between you and other people than for you to send them, or even attempt to send them, a new customer. They will like you and remember you forever.

Become a Joiner

Most people who join associations show up for the meetings, pass out their business cards, and leave either before or as soon as the meeting is over. But that's not for you.

Instead, read the association's literature or guidebook and identify the most important committees. Volunteer for service on one of those committees. Attend the committee meetings and offer to perform tasks and do things that the committee needs done.

It turns out that the most important people in an association sit on the most important committees. When you offer to serve on a committee, volunteer for responsibilities, and then fulfill your responsibilities quickly and well, you get an opportunity to "perform" in a nonthreatening way in front of people who can be of great help to you in your career. People get an opportunity to see the kind of person you are and the kind of work you do. They make mental notes. They store away these mental notes and start to think about opportunities that they could open up for you, jobs they could hire you for, or friends they can recommend who need someone with your talents and abilities.

Every day, thousands of important jobs are filled by recommendations from someone who served on the committee of a voluntary or nonprofit organization. My own personal career was helped enormously with this strategy.

Invest Your Time Well

Average people, with little future, go home and watch television every night. Top people, with great futures ahead of them, network approximately two nights per week. These two nights often save them years of hard work in reaching a desired position in their fields.

ACTION EXERCISES

1. Network continually, everywhere you go, even at restaurants and in theater lines. Introduce yourself to people, ask what they do, and listen attentively to their answers.

2. Resolve today to join at least one association whose members you can help and who can help you in your business. These organizations are always open and eager to welcome new members.

FOURTEEN

Knowledge Is Power

BECOME AN *EXPERT* in your field. Become the most knowledgeable person in your area at your company. Develop a reputation as the best in your business.

We are living in the information age, and you are a knowledge worker. The quality and quantity of the knowledge that you can apply to get results for your company and for other people determines your value, your income, and your future prospects more than anything else.

Expert power exists in every organization. It accrues to people who have their business knowledge down cold. To get this power you must learn everything you can about your job. Take the time to read the books, attend the courses, and learn your job inside out.

Lessons from Fastest-Growing Companies

Each year, *Inc.* magazine publishes a list of the 500 fastest-growing companies in America. (In 2014, the fastest-growing company grew more than 42,000 percent from the previous three years!) The magazine conducted a survey and asked the companies, "What would be the best place for a business to invest money if it wanted to increase sales and profitability faster?"

You may be surprised at the answer. It was not to increase the advertising, improve the packaging, or develop a new competitive strategy. Instead, the best investment was to *improve the quality* of the product or service. Fast-growing companies agreed that this would have more of an impact on sales and profitability than any other use of the same amount of money.

Quality Improvement = Success

This is really not surprising. The most profitable companies are those that are recognized as being the highest-quality providers to their particular customers in their markets. Even Walmart, whose customers are the 70 percent of the population who live from paycheck to paycheck, is considered the highest-quality provider for those people in terms of offering them the widest range of products and services at the most competitive prices.

This principle of quality improvement applies to you as well. The very best investment of your time and money is back into *yourself*—to upgrade your knowledge and skills and increase the quality of your work. Nothing has a higher payoff, or is more guaranteed to lead to greater success, than for you to become known as one of the top people in your field.

Develop a Long-Term Strategy

In their book *Competing for the Future*, Gary Hamel and C. K. Prahalad pointed out that the strategy of successful companies was to project forward five years and identify the core competencies that the company would have to have to lead its field sometime in the future—and then begin today to develop those competencies.

For you to lead your field, you must identify the essential knowledge and skills that you will have to have in the future to be known as the best in your industry. What are they?

The wonderful discovery is that the more you learn, the more you can learn. The smarter you get, the smarter you get. The better your memory, the faster your memory improves. Each time you learn something new, you activate more of your brain cells, which makes it even easier for you to learn more things in the future.

Study the Highest-Paid People

Look around you in your business or industry and identify the highest-paid people. Who are they and what special knowledge and skills do they have that cause them to stand out from others?

According to *BusinessWeek*, the average CEO of a Fortune 500 company earns $10.3 million a year. This is an average of

258 times the average salary of the people who work in their companies. How could this be?

The answer is that these top executives accumulated essential skills, one by one, over the course of their careers. Each of these skills, in combination with other skills, enabled them to get better and better results, faster and faster. The impact of a highly competent CEO can be billions of dollars in increased profitability over the course of a year. When compared with this positive return, an average salary of $10.3 million is easily affordable and easily justifiable.

Identify the Key Skills You Need

What specific skills do you need to develop to become one of the most valuable people in your business? Just one new idea that you are able to glean from reading and studying can be worth a fortune to your business if it is the right idea at the right time.

Become an expert *quietly*. Make a decision that you are going to be one of the top 5 percent of people in your field. Learn until you reach the point that no one knows your business better than you do.

Never tell all you know. This doesn't mean that you withhold information. Just don't wear your knowledge on your sleeve or present your expertise as if you were a know-it-all. Simply focus on becoming a more valuable resource to your organization, getting better and better, week by week, in those areas that can most contribute to revenues and profitability in your organization.

You have heard it said that knowledge is power. Actually, the truth is that only *practical* knowledge is power. Knowledge needs to be applied to some good purpose to get improved results. All the rest is theory.

ACTION EXERCISES

1. Select the one skill or competence that can make you more valuable to your business than any other skill, and then commit yourself wholeheartedly to mastering that skill.

2. Identify the one skill, the lack of which is holding you back from realizing your full potential, and resolve to develop that skill as well. (Sometimes they are the same skills.)

FIFTEEN

Dress for Success

PEOPLE JUDGE you by the way you look on the outside. Ninety-five percent of the first impression that you make on other people comes from your dress and grooming. This is because your clothing and hair covers 95 percent of what other people can see.

Dress for success. Look at the top people in your organization and use them as your models. People are not comfortable working with or promoting others who are different. Emulate the best examples and the top people in your organization and your industry. If they dress in a particular style, then adopt that style. Be knowledgeable about the dress codes in your company and don't violate them.

Some say, "People shouldn't judge me by the way I look on the outside." But the fact is that you judge *everyone else* by the way they look on the outside, so why shouldn't they judge you the same way, which they are going to do anyway.

How My Life Changed

My success was slow in coming. I was knowledgeable and well prepared. I was positive, pleasant, and personable when I met with customers. But somehow, at the moment of decision, they would almost always say, "Well, let me think about it."

Then one day something happened that changed my life. An older, wiser, and much more successful salesman took me aside and kindly asked me if I would be open to a little feedback on my way of dressing. I was hungry to learn, so I told him that I would take any advice he could offer.

At that time, I was wearing a cheap, ill-fitting suit that I had bought in a small tailor shop at a low price. And it looked it, too. In combination with a wash-and-wear rayon shirt, a thin tie, scruffy shoes, and long hair, I did not inspire confidence in anyone, especially customers.

I still remember this man giving me a tutorial on proper business dress. He told me about cuffs, lapels, shirt collars, and fit. He explained to me the importance of matching different colors with each other and the need for more expensive and polished shoes.

A New Wardrobe

Over the next few days, he took me out and helped me piece together a new wardrobe, which I could barely afford.

The first day that I began calling on prospects wearing my new outfit, the reaction was extraordinary. Instead of people treating me like a low-level salesman who had just come in from the street, prospective customers addressed me with great respect and listened carefully to what I said. Best of all, they began to buy from me, more and more. I was soon making more money than I had ever made in my life.

Proper Business Dress Opens Doors

Buy and read at least one book on proper business attire and follow it closely. Your wardrobe is too important to neglect. I have had situations in my career where the very fact that I was the best-dressed executive in the office brought me opportunities. The reason is simple: *Credibility is everything.*

A well-dressed person looks more competent and seems smarter and more believable in a work environment. People tend to trust your judgment more when you look excellent in every respect.

Accessories and other details are important as well, including belts, ties, jewelry, socks, and shoes. Keep your briefcase or handbag clean, attractive, and in good repair.

Grooming is very important. When people look at your face, they see your hair, your head, and your neck. They make an immediate decision about whether you are credible.

Human beings are subject to what is called "confirmation bias." They form their first opinion of you within four seconds of meeting you for the first time. Over the next thirty seconds, they finalize their initial opinion. After that, they look for proof to confirm what they have already decided to believe about you. This is why they say that it is very hard to make a second first impression. It is too late.

Political Advice

When I was advising political candidates, I discovered the importance of facial hair. At an unconscious level, men who wear beards are considered to be hiding something, like a robber wearing a mask. The first unconscious impression you have when you meet a man wearing a beard in a business situation is that this person cannot be trusted.

If a person wears a mustache, they are considered to be indecisive. They cannot make a decision between a mustache, a full beard, or nothing.

The first advice we give a political candidate with a beard is to shave it off. The first advice we give a salesperson, lawyer, or anyone else who wishes to influence others, is to get rid of the facial hair.

Look Like a Champion

Every morning, look at yourself in the mirror and ask, "Do I look like the very best people in my business?"

What kind of an impression do you make on people when they see you for the first time? If you are not happy with your answer, or you are not happy with the initial impression you are making, remember that the impression you make is totally under your own control. You choose and arrange every item of your clothing and your grooming every single morning.

ACTION EXERCISES

1. Look around you at the most successful and respected people in your field. How do you dress in comparison to them?

2. Spend twice as much money and buy half as many clothes. Purchase one excellent outfit that makes you look like a million dollars. Wear it to work and see what happens.

SIXTEEN

Commit to Excellence

BE THE BEST in your field. Superior performance is the foundation of all rapid advancement, in any job. Commit to excellence at what you do. Set high standards for yourself and refuse to compromise them for any reason.

There are two wars going on in the world of work today. There is the war of performance vs. the war of politics. You must choose the first one and decide to win on that ground.

Avoid Political Gamesmanship

There are some people who are excellent at office politics, at least for a short time. They are referred to as the Machiavellians. It turns out that people who focus on politics usually mask the poor quality of their work. They are eventually found out. Those who focus on performance, on doing a good job and getting better and better at their work, are the ones who eventually win out in the end.

The Machiavellians, the politicians, are inevitably bypassed in the long game by the performers. This is because an organization only survives to the degree to which it attracts and rewards high-performing men and women. In the long run, the politicians do not contribute to the success of the organization. If you have a choice, focus all of your energy on performance.

Peter Drucker said, "The man or woman who is excellent in his or her field, [who] is a high performer and does quality work, is above politics."

This doesn't mean that you ignore politics; it just means that superior performance is the real key to promotion.

Regarding rapid promotion, researchers have found over and over again that contacts, politics, money, education, and experience are completely discarded in assessing performance. When you become a high performer, you won't have to worry about anything or anyone else.

Three Factors to Consider

In developing a personal business model, a model that you can use to move to the top of your field, there are three factors you need to consider: what, who, and how.

KNOW YOUR VALUE OFFERING

The "what" refers to your *value offering*. What is it you do that makes you invaluable and even indispensable to your company? What *could* you do if you were to develop new skills and abilities? What skills *should* you develop for the future?

Your value offering is a summary statement of the value you contribute that can justify somebody hiring you and paying you the kind of money you want and even more in the future. What value do you bring to your business?

FOCUS ON YOUR CUSTOMER

The "who" is the customer, the person you serve, the customer who must utilize and benefit from your special talents and skills. Usually this customer is the boss, but often the customer will be your coworkers, your staff, and the external customers using your company's products or services.

What you are looking for is that perfect point where your special skills connect exactly with the specific needs of the person who most benefits from the results that you can get with those skills.

DELIVER RESULTS

The "how" of your personal business model is the way that you deliver results that people want, need, can use, and will pay for. Your ability to focus single-mindedly on one result at a time, the most important result, and to achieve it quickly and well, is what enables you to rise to the top of your field.

Attract Attention

Excellent performance will always bring you to the attention of your superiors, usually faster than anything else. Performance is everything.

In studies, researchers have found that no matter what college you graduated from (or whether you even graduated from college) or what kind of grades you got, two years into your career, *nobody cares*. Two years after you start work, all anybody cares about is how good you are at what you do.

We spoke about the importance of investing in quality in your products and services in Chapter 14. This is equally true for you *personally*. The more you invest your time and effort to become better and better at what you do, the more doors will open for you and the faster they will open.

ACTION EXERCISES

1. Identify the one area where excellent performance can help you make the most valuable contribution to your company, and dedicate yourself to becoming excellent in that area.

2. Identify the areas where you are not particularly good and in which you have little interest, and look for ways to delegate those activities to others so that you have more time to do the few things that will make the greatest difference in your career.

SEVENTEEN

Plan Strategically

THE ABILITY to plan strategically is a key skill for success in business and personal life. In fact, the ability to think strategically, to play down the chessboard of life, is essential to your success.

Become a good strategic planner. Plan months and even years ahead. Take time to think about where you want to be in the long term and make sure that everything you are doing today is moving you in that direction.

The Strategic Planning Process

There is a simple seven-part strategic planning process that you can apply to your life and work.

1. *Your vision.* Imagine that there are no limitations on what you can be, have, and do in the years ahead. If your career was *perfect* five years from now, what would it look like, and how would it be different from today?

2. *Your values.* What are your most important values in life, and in what order of importance do they exist for you? The greater *clarity* you have about your true values, the easier it is for you to make important decisions.

3. *Your mission.* This is what you want to do to bring about a positive change in the life and work of other people. Remember, we all make our living by serving other people in some way. What is your mission?

4. *Your purpose.* This is the reason you get out of bed in the morning. It is the reason you do what you are currently doing rather than something else. What is your "why" in life?

5. *Your goals.* These are the specific, written, measurable, time-bounded goals that you want to achieve sometime in the future, based on your values, vision, mission, and purpose. What are they?

6. *Your priorities.* These are the most important things you do each day. Your ability to set priorities, to determine the most valuable use of your time relative to achieving your goals, is the key to high performance.

7. *Your actions.* These are the actions you take to achieve your highest priorities. Determine the specific actions that you need to take immediately to accomplish your highest priorities and achieve your goals.

Think On Paper

All successful men and women are planners. They write things down continually, and in detail. Thinking on paper is an important principle of success.

Think through your goals and those of your unit or department, and consider the *consequences* of various plans of action. A hallmark of high intelligence is the ability to anticipate the secondary or long-term consequences of your current actions. What is likely to happen?

Continually ask the questions:

"What am I trying to do?"

"How am I trying to do it?"

"Could there be a better way?"

In planning strategically, always be open to the possibility that you are on the wrong track, that there could be a *better way* to accomplish a specific result or to achieve your goals.

Once you have created your strategic plan, you must set your priorities, focus on high-value tasks, and then concentrate your unique talents and skills in those areas that can make a significant difference.

ACTION EXERCISES

1. If your business or career was perfect sometime in the future, what would it look like, and how would it be different from today?

2. Identify the specific, measurable, time-sensitive actions that you can take immediately to create your ideal future.

EIGHTEEN

Accept Responsibility for Results

ONE OF THE qualities of peak performers is that they accept 100 percent responsibility for their work. This is vitally important. This means "no excuses and no blaming."

Never complain and never explain. If things don't go well, accept responsibility for the situation and take action to change or improve it. The acceptance of personal responsibility is the mark of the leader. It is the turning point in a person's life and career. It is the difference between childhood and maturity.

An Attitude of Ownership

In a survey done in New York, the top 3 percent of people in various professions had one attitude in common. No matter what field or company these people worked in, they all saw themselves as self-employed. They acted as if they owned the place. They looked upon themselves as though they were the personal owners of their companies, and no matter who signed their paychecks, they were in complete charge of their own careers.

They spoke in terms of "we" and "us" and "our," rather than "they" and "them," as most people do. They worked longer hours and took more responsibility for the results of the company and any success or lack of success that the company experienced.

There is nothing that makes a manager or an employer happier than to see employees who really care about their company and show an attitude of ownership in everything they do. If a manager or an executive had to promote someone and one candidate looked at the job as just a job and the other candidate looked at the company as if it belonged to him, the hiring executive would always choose to promote the person that takes full responsibility for the results of the organization.

If things go wrong or you make a mistake, simply admit it. Say, "I was wrong. I blew it." Then focus on what you can learn from the experience.

All human beings make mistakes. But always take responsibility for the mistake and for finding a solution to it. Always say, "What is our next action?"

No One Is Perfect

In most cases, the people around you will already know when you make a mistake. When you have the courage and character to admit to it, they will admire and respect you more. Taking responsibility for a mistake raises your level of credibility and increases the respect you garner from those around you.

It turns out that *positive emotions* are the key to success in life. The major obstacle to positive emotions is *negative emotions.* If you can eliminate negative emotions, all that will be left are the positive emotions that are life-enhancing.

The great discovery is that negative emotions are almost always triggered by blame. They are caused by the failure to accept responsibility for your situation. Whenever you blame someone for anything, you feel negative, unhappy, inferior, and small.

Feeling Powerful and Purposeful

On the other hand, whenever you accept responsibility, you feel powerful, purposeful, and self-confident. The secret is simple—simply say the magic words "I am responsible!" whenever anything goes wrong. Whenever you have a negative thought or emotion, immediately cancel it out by saying, "I am responsible!"

It is impossible to accept responsibility and to be negative at the same time. The one emotion, that of responsibility, eliminates the other emotion, that of blame, and makes you a completely positive person.

ACTION EXERCISES

1. Think of a situation in your life or work that makes you angry or unhappy. Cancel your feelings about that situation

by immediately saying "I am responsible!" Say these words over and over again until the negative situation loses its power over you.

2. Never blame anyone for anything or try to make a person feel bad for a past event or a mistake. Instead, say, "Next time, let's do it this way." And move on.

NINETEEN

Be a Team Player

ONE OF THE most important qualities for advancement in any organization is the ability to function well as part of a team. It is the key quality required if you want to be promoted to the executive suite. Executives require the ability to organize, work with others, and coordinate a team of people with different skills and abilities.

Virtually everything in the world of work is accomplished as the result of two or more people working together, with overlapping roles and responsibilities. It stands to reason, then, that one of the major obstacles to promotion is the inability to work or cooperate with teams of other people.

The Five Keys
There are five key elements that have been identified in the building of peak performance teams.

1. *Shared goals and objectives.* Top teams take the time to agree on the goals and objectives of the team. They set clear measures for the goal and measures for each person on the team.

2. *Shared values.* Team members discuss and agree on the values and principles that they will use to interact with each other. These values include punctuality, responsibility, the need to complete assignments on time, and so on.

3. *Shared plans of action.* Team members discuss and agree upon exactly what each one of them is going to do to help achieve the overall goal, when they are going to do it, and how it will be measured.

4. *One leader.* There is always a team leader, the person who is ultimately responsible. One person leads the action. The leader's job is to make sure that all other team members have the resources they need to do their jobs correctly and on time.

5. *Continuous review and evaluation.* The team meets regularly to discuss how well they are doing in achieving the objective, how satisfied the customers are with the product or service, and how well the team is working together as a group.

When you practice these five principles, you can build a high-performing team quickly. These principles are responsible for some of the greatest accomplishments in the world of business.

Seek Opportunities to Contribute

Instead of looking at how much you can get, always look at how much you can give. Focus on contribution and cooperation. Be a helper. Dedicate yourself to making a valuable contribution to the team, and be supportive of others.

Give credit to others for successes. The more you give credit away to others, the more credit you will end up getting. The leader always accepts the responsibility for problems, but gives the credit away to the team members for successes and accomplishments.

When you start off in business, your ability to be a valuable team member is the first rung on the ladder to success. As you contribute more and more value, the faster you will become a team leader. You will have more people to help you achieve bigger and bigger goals. The better you perform as a team leader, the greater your responsibilities for results and the faster you will be promoted.

ACTION EXERCISES

1. Determine the exact goals and objectives of your team, and set clear measures for everyone on the achievement of those goals and objectives.

2. Discuss, decide, and agree on the values of your team. Determine how you will work and interact together and how you will solve problems.

TWENTY

Develop Your Creativity

ONE OF THE greatest enemies of success is the comfort zone. It is amazing how many people become comfortable doing things in a certain way and then resist all change, no matter how helpful or positive it might be.

Machiavelli once wrote: "There is nothing more difficult to take in hand, more perilous to conduct, or more uncertain in its success, than to take the lead in the introduction of a new order of things. For the innovator will have only the mild support of those who would benefit, and the vigorous opposition of all those whose positions are threatened."

Innovation Is Essential

The more you do of what you're doing, the more you'll get of what you've got. All success comes from moving out of your comfort zone, trying something new or different, taking risks and accepting the fact that most things don't work out, at the least the first time you try them.

The good news is that there is a direct relationship between the quantity of your ideas and the quality of your success. Every business today rises or falls on the basis of the flow of new ideas, new products, new services, new processes, and new approaches to doing things.

Better, Cheaper, Faster

Always be looking for ways to accomplish your goals in ways that are better, faster, or cheaper. Every business is aimed at making profits. The only way to make profits is to increase sales and revenues or to lower costs and expenses. The best is to do both at the same time.

Every idea that you can come up with that will increase your revenues or lower your costs will bring you to the attention of people who can help you move ahead faster.

Once you get a good idea, you need to do several things. First is to check it out. Do some research. Get the facts. Find out for sure before you commit. Once you are convinced that you have a good idea, put it on paper. Write it out. Create a proposal and offer it to your boss or to whomever's agreement is necessary to implement it.

Expect a Negative Reaction

Most people say *no* to any new idea. This is neither positive nor negative. It is just the way people are, even though they recognize that they need new and better ideas.

The key is to offer your idea tentatively, and then ask other people for their opinions. Say something like, "I had this idea to cut our costs (or increase our sales). I have checked into it and I think there might be something to it. What do you think?"

Don't try to sell your idea or worry about getting credit, at least for the moment. Just seek another opinion. Ask the magic question, "What do you think?"

Be Patient

When you present a new idea, never ask for an immediate decision. Instead, encourage your boss to look it over and think about it for a while.

Many years ago, a mentor of mine, the president of a large organization with more than 10,000 employees, gave me a gift. It was a yellowed pamphlet, many years old, titled *Take Time Out for Mental Digestion.*

He told me that this little pamphlet had shaped and guided his entire career and was largely responsible for his success in taking over and running large businesses. The pamphlet had a simple premise. It said that it is natural and normal for the human mind to reject new ideas. Therefore, when you present something new or different, always give the other person at least seventy-two hours to think about it. Let people digest the idea. Let them turn the idea over in their own minds and evaluate it for themselves.

Suggest a Pilot Project

Another way to introduce a new idea, especially if there is a large amount of skepticism or resistance, is to suggest a test project. Offer to try it out on a small scale. Reduce the amount of time, money, and risk involved by offering to invest your own time to find out if your idea has any merit.

You will almost always get approval for a small test. With the results of your small test, you can come back and make a case for implementing your idea on a larger scale.

Most New Ideas Don't Work

In advertising, they say that there are three keys to success: Test, test, test.

It is the same with new ideas. Most new ideas do not work the first time, and often the first few times. But as you test, get reactions and responses, learn lessons, and test again, you will often come up with a breakthrough idea that can really help your company and boost your career.

Keep On Going

No matter what the boss's reaction or response, keep coming up with new ideas. Even if you get turned down, remember that there is a direct relationship between the number of good ideas that you generate and the rate at which you move ahead in your career. It is almost as if ideas are a form of super fuel in the tank of your success. The more ideas you have, the faster you will move ahead, even if your ideas are not successful initially.

ACTION EXERCISES

1. Identify the biggest problem or obstacle to increasing sales and profitability in your business. Then, make a list of ten to twenty ways that you could solve this problem and boost your sales and profits.

2. When you get a good idea, keep it to yourself. Instead of telling others, do your homework. Gather information. Make a case for your idea based on independent research and personal testing.

TWENTY-ONE

Put Fortune on Your Side

WHEN I TOOK my executive MBA program many years ago, I was required to take a course on probability theory. I had failed high school and only gotten into the MBA program because I had a high SAT score. My worst subject in school had been mathematics, and probability theory was based on differential calculus, complex ways of evaluating data and determining probabilities.

I was so bad at probability theory that I had to repeat the course two semesters in a row before I got through it. But it turned out to be one of the most valuable programs I had ever attended. It changed my life forever.

The Invaluable Lesson

What I learned in probability theory was that there is a probability that anything and everything can happen, and these probabilities can be calculated with great precision by using one of the many formulas that has been developed over the last 300 years. I also learned that our entire world is based on probability theory. All stocks and stock market reports, all insurance and actuarial tables, all science, mathematics, physics, and many of the Nobel Prizes that have been awarded as the result of new discoveries in economics are based on probability theory.

The Probabilities of Success

Here is the point. There is a probability that you are going to be a big success in your career. There is a probability that you are going to become a millionaire, or better, in the course of your working lifetime. Your great business throughout your lifetime is to increase the probabilities that you are the right person, at the right time, who enjoys the great successes that are possible for you. And this is largely under your control.

INCREASE THE PROBABILITIES

There are seven ways that you can increase the probabilities that you are going to realize your full potential and become everything that you are capable of becoming.

1. *Make a decision to go to the top of your field.* Most people never do this. They long for greater success. They admire people who are more successful than themselves. They yearn for greater income and responsibilities. But they never make a firm decision that they are going to go to the top.

Refuse to settle for anything less than excellence. Remember that there are very few limits on what you can do if you make a firm decision and then back it up with continuous action.

2. *Set clear, specific, written goals for your career.* Create a checklist, a blueprint. Work on your goals every day.

3. *Focus on contribution.* Concentrate on creating value and generating revenue for your business. Forget about politics. Instead, let your performance speak for you.

4. *Accept 100 percent responsibility for everything you are and everything you do.* Step up. Volunteer. Ask for more responsibility and then do whatever is given you to do with speed and dependability.

5. *Look for moments when you can shine.* When you get an opportunity to contribute and to do more work, look upon it as an opportunity to demonstrate your ability and to prove to others why you should be paid more and promoted faster.

6. *Identify your "limiting skill" to success.* It turns out that your weakest important skill sets the height or limit on your success. The areas in which you are proficient are what have gotten you to where you are today. Your weakest key skill, however, is the brake on your performance. It is what holds you back more than anything else. Make a decision, right now, whatever that limiting skill might be, to master that skill in the months ahead.

7. *Resolve in advance that you will never give up.* You will persist, night and day, until you are the big success that you are truly capable of becoming.

Use the Law on Your Behalf

The Law of Probability is not a theory, principle, or an idea. It is a *law*. It works for everyone, at all times. The rule is that the more you try, the more you will triumph. The more things you do, the longer and harder you work, the more likely it is that you will do the right things at the right times that will open the right doors that will accelerate your career. And this will not be a matter of luck or chance, but of law.

ACTION EXERCISES

1. Sit down with a piece of paper and set clear, specific goals for your career. Decide exactly where you want to be in one month, six months, one year, and in two and five years. Do not leave your career to chance.

2. Identify the one skill that might be holding you back from realizing far more of your potential. Ask your boss. Ask your coworkers. But be clear about what it is, and then make a decision to master that skill. Remember, all skills are *learnable*. You can learn any skill you need to learn to achieve any goal that you set for yourself.

Three Keys to Success

SUCCESS IS NOT an accident. It is completely predictable. If you do what other successful people have done before you, by the Law of Cause and Effect, you will soon get the results that other people get. And if you don't, you won't.

There are three keys to success that have been learned and unlearned, discovered and rediscovered throughout the ages. They are all learnable through practice and repetition.

The Power of Self-Discipline

Number one, which underlines everything we've talked about, is self-discipline. Be willing to pay the price for success in advance.

As you have read these success principles, you have probably identified one or more areas of personal weakness that could be holding you back. And the great tragedy in life is that nobody will tell you or point out to you this weakness. They will let you struggle with it for years.

Sometimes, if you work slowly and think you are doing a really good job by being careful and meticulous, you may find that because of a perceived lack of urgency you are being bypassed for promotion and rewards. You may find that by speeding up a little, without diminishing the quality of your work, your rewards will increase. Discipline is essential.

Proven Success Methods

Number two is to use proven success methods. Use the ideas that we have discussed in this book. If you sense that you have a weakness in goal setting, time management, creative thinking, decision making, communications, or public speaking, study the experts. Learn from the masters. Go to school, take courses, and read books. You can learn anything you need to know to be successful.

Ask Your Way

Number three is to "ask" your way to success. If you ask enough people in the right way, they will tell you what you need to learn, where to find it, and how to use it to be successful.

Start with your boss. Ask if your boss sees any weaknesses in you that you can compensate for. Look around for different courses and books that can help you. Start building your own personal success library. Buy or download audio learning programs and listen to them each day. Remember, the clock is ticking. The race is on. And this life is not a rehearsal for something else.

Finally, develop the unshakable determination, resolve, and willingness to persist until you succeed, and if you do, nothing can stop you.

You Are the Architect of Your Own Destiny

In the final analysis, if you are willing to work on yourself, to build and improve yourself, and to work systematically every single day toward your goals and the personal success you desire, the Law of Accumulation says that gradually and inexorably your efforts will build, accumulate, and develop into an exceptional life.

No one achieves success overnight. Success is always a result of hundreds and thousands of small efforts and achievements that nobody ever notices or appreciates. Make a decision, this very day, to practice these ideas, over and over again, until they become habits, until they become easy and an automatic way of living for you. When you do, there will be no limits.

accumulation, law of, 3, 103

"act as if," 17

action, 83
   anticipating consequences of current, 84
   bias for, 34–37
   orientation, 36
   toward goal, 13

action plan, shared, 90

Allen, David, *Getting Things Done*, 35

Angelou, Maya, 24

anticipating consequences of current actions, 84

Aristotle, 4

associations, joining, 66

attention, attracting, 80–81

attitude
   controlling, 26–27
   of ownership, 85–86

attraction, law of, 6–7

beards, 76

Becker, Gary, 49

belief, law of, 5–6

bias for action, 34–37

BNI (Business Network International), 64

boss
   expectations of, 32
   help from, 102
   as main customer, 39–40

business associations, 64

business dress, 74–75

business success, 41

BusinessWeek, 70

career goals, identifying, 11

caring, 20

Carnegie Institute of Technology, 27

causality, principle of, 4

cause-and-effect, 4

CEOs, studying, 70–71

challenge, vs. problem, 30

checklist, for goal, 13

Churchill, Winston, 15

clarity, 10–11

comfort zone, 92

commitment to excellence, 78–81

committees, in associations, 66

communication, positive, 29–33

competence, 2

Competing for the Future (Hamel and Prahalad), 70

confirmation bias, 75–76

continuous learning, 48–52

contribution, 99
   focus on, 91, 99

correspondence, law of, 7–8

courage, 15–18

coworkers, as customers, 40–41

creativity, 92–96

credibility, 75
credit to others, 91
customers
    focus on, 80
    identifying, 38–39
    satisfying important, 38–42

Dale Carnegie Training office, 55
Danko, William, *The Millionaire Next Door*, 44
deadline for goal, 13
decisions, on what you want, 10–14
dress, for success, 73–77
Drucker, Peter, 19, 35, 79
Dyer, Wayne, 5

80/20 rule, 49–50
Einstein, Albert, 38
elite performance, achieving, 3
Emerson, Ralph Waldo, 16, 21
emotions, positive or negative, 87
Ericsson, K. Anders, 3
excellence, commitment to, 78–81
expectations, positive, 31–33
expert, becoming, 71
expert power, 68
explanatory style, 29–31

facial hair, 76
family goals, 11–12
fears
    of failure, 16
    moving toward, 16–17
    overcoming, 54
    short-circuiting, 56
    unlearning, 16
first opinions, 75–76
focal point, 14
focus
    on contribution, 91
    on results, 35
Foster, David, 45

Getting Things Done (Allen), 35
goals, 83, 93, 99
    identifying, 11–12
    selecting ten, 13–14
    seven-step process for setting, 12–13
    shared, 90
grooming, 75

Hamel, Gary, *Competing for the Future*, 70
happiness, 18
    source of, 12
health, 18
help, from boss, 102
Hill, Napoleon, 14
    Think and Grow Rich, 59
honor, 22–23
hours of work, 45
Hubbard, Elbert, 54–55
Hunt, H.L., 10

Inc. magazine, 69
income earners, top 20 percent, 50
inequality, 45
inner dialogue, 29–31
inner voice, 21
innovation, 92–93
integrity, 19–23
intelligence, and success, 1–2
intuition, trust in, 21
inverse paranoid, 32

James, William, 16
jobs, creative search, 64

knowledge, 68–72

laws, 4–9
    Law of Accumulation, 3, 103
    Law of Attraction, 6–7
    Law of Belief, 5–6

laws *(continued)*
    Law of Correspondence, 7–8
    Law of Probability, 100
leader, of team, 90
learning, continuous, 48–52
lessons, from setback, 26
limiting skill to success, 99
listening, 51
Longfellow, Henry Wadsworth, 3
long-term strategy, 70

Machiavelli, Niccolò, 92
Machiavellians, 78–79
Mandino, Og, 34
mastermind concept, 59–61
McClelland, David, 58
McPherson, James, 15
mental laws, 5
millionaire, self-made, 43–44
The Millionaire Next Door (Stanley
    and Danko), 44
mind, feeding continually, 26
mission, 83
mistakes, 86–87
mustache, 76

natural laws, 5
negative beliefs, 6
negative emotions, 87
negative reaction, 93
networking, 63–67
neutrality, 5
new ideas, 95
Nightingale, Earl, 21

opportunity, 30, 35–36
optimism, 31
    learned, 25–27
others, need for, 27
ownership, attitude of, 85–86

paranoid, 32

Pareto principle, 2
patience, 94
peer group, choice of, 58–62
personal business model, factors to
    consider, 79–80
personal goals, 11–12
pilot project, 95
planning, strategic, 82–84
planning, strategic, on paper, 84
political gamesmanship, 78–79
positive attitude, 24–28
positive beliefs, 6
positive emotions, 87
positive expectations, 31–33
positive self-talk, 30
power, 87
Prahalad, C.K., *Competing for the
    Future*, 70
principle of causality, 4
priority, 36–37, 83
probability theory, 97–98
    and success, 98–-100
problem, vs. challenge, 30
promises, 21–22
purpose, 83, 87
purposeful action, 14

quality improvement, success and,
    69–70
questions, for networking, 65

random events, 4
reaction, negative, 93
reading every day, 50–51
reference group, 58
rejection, fear of, and fear of public
    speaking, 56
reputation, 19–23
responsibility, 99
results, delivering, 80
Robert Half & Associates, 46
Rosenthal, David, 31

Rothschild, Baron de, 61

self, promises to, 22
self-confidence, 15–18
self-discipline, power of, 101–102
self-employed, 86
self-limiting beliefs, 6
self-made millionaire, 43–44
    common denominator, 44–45
self-talk, positive, 30
Seligman, Martin, 25
Shakespeare, William, 20, 24
skills, identifying needed, 71
speaking, 53–57
    getting started, 55
    overcoming fear, 54
spouse, expectations of, 32
staff
    as customers, 40–41
    expectations of, 32
Stanley, Thomas, *The Millionaire
    Next Door*, 44
Stone, W. Clement, 32
strategic planning, 82–84
strategy, long-term, 70
subconscious, programming, 31
success
    dress for, 73–77
    Hunt on, 10
    keys to, 101–103
    masterminds and, 60
    probability theory and, 98–100

proven methods, 102
quality improvement and,
    69–70
reasons for, 1–2
systematic desensitization, 55

Take Time Out for Mental Digestion
    (pamphlet), 94
tasks, 36
    completion, 34
team players, 89–91
Think and Grow Rich (Hill), 59
thinking, 8
    impact of change, 7
time, use of, 46, 67
Toastmasters International, 55

training, 51–52
trust, in intuition, 21

value offering, 79–80
values, 83
    personal, 20
    shared, 90
vision, 82–83

winning edge concept, 2–3
work, engaged with, 20
working time, waste of, 46
writing goals, 12

Ziglar, Zig, 59